My Journey To Recovery

A 60-Day Guided Journal For Women Recovering From Cosmetic Surgery

KRYSTLE MAY PENN

ISBN: 979-8-9892142-0-4 (Paperback)
ISBN: 979-8-9892142-1-1 (Digital copy)

Printed by Krystle Clear Wellness, LLC, in the USA.

First printing edition, 2023.

Krystle Clear Wellness, LLC
1445 Woodmont Ln NW #2841
Atlanta GA 30318

DEDICATION

To the brave and resilient women on their path to recovery from post-op cosmetic surgery. May you find unwavering strength and inspiration within the pages of this journal as you transform with grace, confidence, and boundless positivity.

Thank you for entrusting me with the privilege of being part of your healing journey. Please don't hesitate to reach out—I'm here to support you every step of the way.

With love and admiration,

Krystle May B. Penn

Sept. 11, 2023

INTRODUCTION

Hello, dear reader,

Let me welcome you to this transformative journey. My name is Krystle May Penn, and I am a certified manual lymphatic drainage therapist. I stand before you, not just as the author of this journal, but as someone who has witnessed first-hand, the challenges women face through post-op cosmetic recovery. Their transformation is not just physical, but mental and emotional as well.

In my journey as a massage therapist, I have come to realize the profound importance of self-care. I've seen how easily we neglect our own self-care amidst the demands of life and the desire to heal quickly. We often dedicate ourselves entirely to the well-being of others, whether it's through our careers or our personal lives. However, we sometimes forget that our own well-being is equally essential. It was this realization that inspired me to create this sixty-day guided journal for women recovering from post-operative cosmetic surgery.

Through the coming sixty days, you will find prompts, reflections, and exercises tailored to your unique needs as you heal and grow. This journal is your space to celebrate your progress, acknowledge your challenges, and embrace your inner strength. It is also my commitment for both you and myself. It's an embodiment of the belief that self-care is not a luxury but a necessity, especially during this pivotal time in your life. It's a reminder that we must take care of ourselves with the same dedication and love we extend to others.

As we enter into this journey together, my hope is that this journal will serve as a guide, a companion, and a source of strength. It's designed to help you nurture your body, mind, and spirit throughout your recovery. But it's also a tool for me, a reminder that I too need to practice what I preach – to prioritize self-care and well-being. Together, let's honor the incredible journey you're on and the courage it takes to embark upon it. Let's commit to better self-care, not just for ourselves but for the ones we care for and the lives we touch.

Example

Recovery Day 1

Date
9 / 30 / 23

HOW I FEEL TODAY

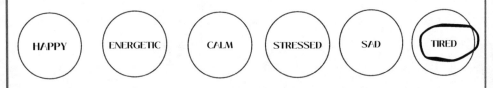

HAPPY · ENERGETIC · CALM · STRESSED · SAD · (TIRED)

SELF-CARE:

- ☑ DID I SLEEP WELL?
- ☐ DID I EAT NOURISHING FOODS?
- ☐ DOES MY COMPRESSION GARMENT FIT NICE & SNUG?
- ☑ ARE MY INCISIONS HEALING PROPERLY?
- ☐ HAS MY MOBILITY IMPROVED TODAY?

MY WATER INTAKE

EACH DROP REPRESENT 16 OUNCES.
80 OUNCES IS RECOMMENDED PER DAY.

NOTES

Very sore. Not much appetite, but I juiced. This thing is really tight. It's hard to move around today.

Reflection

What influenced my decision to undergo cosmetic surgery?

I just wanted to do something for myself. I saw other women doing it. I was really worried about the risks, but I have done extensive research and found some really great doctors.

I am beautiful.

Recovery Day 1

HOW I FEEL TODAY

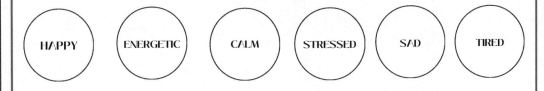

HAPPY   ENERGETIC   CALM   STRESSED   SAD   TIRED

SELF-CARE:

- ☐ DID I SLEEP WELL?

- ☐ DID I EAT NOURISHING FOODS?

- ☐ DOES MY COMPRESSION GARMENT FIT NICE & SNUG?

- ☐ ARE MY INCISIONS HEALING PROPERLY?

- ☐ HAS MY MOBILITY IMPROVED TODAY?

MY WATER INTAKE

EACH DROP REPRESENT 16 OUNCES. 80 OUNCES IS RECOMMENDED PER DAY.

◊◊◊◊◊◊◊

NOTES

Reflection

What influenced my decision to undergo cosmetic surgery?

_____

_____

_____

_____

_____

_____

I love my body.

Recovery Day 2

HOW I FEEL TODAY

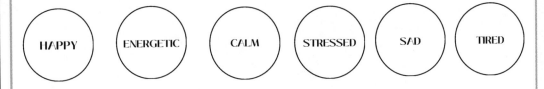

HAPPY ENERGETIC CALM STRESSED SAD TIRED

SELF-CARE:

☐ DID I SLEEP WELL?

☐ DID I EAT NOURISHING FOODS?

☐ DOES MY COMPRESSION GARMENT FIT NICE & SNUG?

☐ ARE MY INCISIONS HEALING PROPERLY?

☐ HAS MY MOBILITY IMPROVED TODAY?

MY WATER INTAKE

EACH DROP REPRESENT 16 OUNCES.
80 OUNCES IS RECOMMENDED PER DAY.

NOTES

Reflection

How can I redefine my own sense of beauty despite any societal pressures/expectations about appearance?

_____

_____

_____

_____

_____

I am vibrant.

Recovery Day 3

HOW I FEEL TODAY

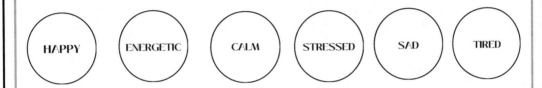

HAPPY | ENERGETIC | CALM | STRESSED | SAD | TIRED

SELF-CARE:

☐ DID I SLEEP WELL?

☐ DID I EAT NOURISHING FOODS?

☐ DOES MY COMPRESSION GARMENT FIT NICE & SNUG?

☐ ARE MY INCISIONS HEALING PROPERLY?

☐ HAS MY MOBILITY IMPROVED TODAY?

MY WATER INTAKE

EACH DROP REPRESENT 16 OUNCES.
80 OUNCES IS RECOMMENDED PER DAY.

NOTES

Reflection

How did you overcome any fears or anxieties about your healing process?

_____

_____

_____

_____

_____

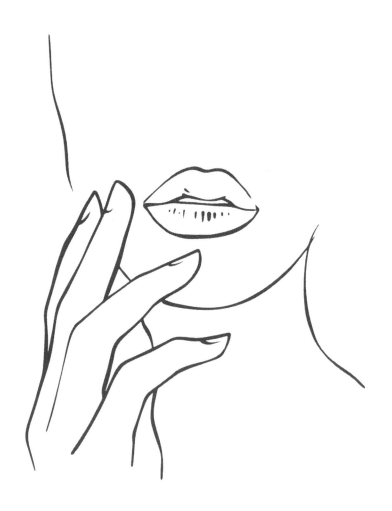

I am capable.

Recovery Day 4

HOW I FEEL TODAY

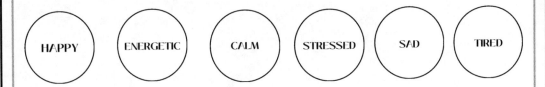

HAPPY   ENERGETIC   CALM   STRESSED   SAD   TIRED

SELF-CARE:

- ☐ DID I SLEEP WELL?

- ☐ DID I EAT NOURISHING FOODS?

- ☐ DOES MY COMPRESSION GARMENT FIT NICE & SNUG?

- ☐ ARE MY INCISIONS HEALING PROPERLY?

- ☐ HAS MY MOBILITY IMPROVED TODAY?

MY WATER INTAKE

*EACH DROP REPRESENT 16 OUNCES.
80 OUNCES IS RECOMMENDED PER DAY.*

NOTES

Reflection

What were your specifications when searching for the right doctor for your procedure?

_____

_____

_____

_____

_____

I am resilient.

Recovery Day 5

HOW I FEEL TODAY

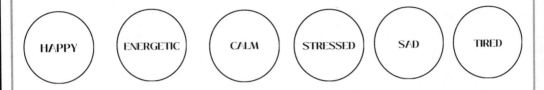

HAPPY   ENERGETIC   CALM   STRESSED   SAD   TIRED

SELF-CARE:

☐ DID I SLEEP WELL?

☐ DID I EAT NOURISHING FOODS?

☐ DOES MY COMPRESSION GARMENT FIT NICE & SNUG?

☐ ARE MY INCISIONS HEALING PROPERLY?

☐ HAS MY MOBILITY IMPROVED TODAY?

MY WATER INTAKE

EACH DROP REPRESENT 16 OUNCES.
80 OUNCES IS RECOMMENDED PER DAY.

◊ ◊ ◊ ◊ ◊ ◊ ◊

NOTES

Reflection

What were some unexpected emotional shifts that you experienced post-surgery? How can you process and understand these changes?

_____

_____

_____

_____

_____

_____

I am grateful.

Recovery Day 6

HOW I FEEL TODAY

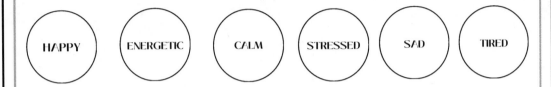

HAPPY ENERGETIC CALM STRESSED SAD TIRED

SELF-CARE:

☐ DID I SLEEP WELL?

☐ DID I EAT NOURISHING FOODS?

☐ DOES MY COMPRESSION GARMENT FIT NICE & SNUG?

☐ ARE MY INCISIONS HEALING PROPERLY?

☐ HAS MY MOBILITY IMPROVED TODAY?

MY WATER INTAKE

EACH DROP REPRESENT 16 OUNCES. 80 OUNCES IS RECOMMENDED PER DAY.

NOTES

Reflection

What new physical changes/improvements did you notice about your body? How can you celebrate these moments of progress?

_____

_____

_____

_____

_____

_____

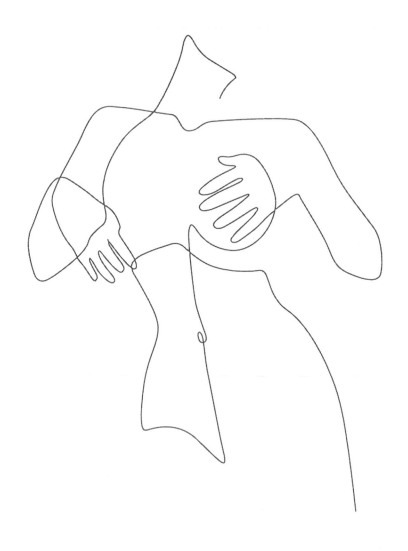

I love every cell in my body.

Recovery Day 7

HOW I FEEL TODAY

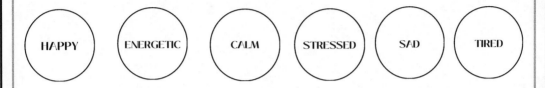

HAPPY   ENERGETIC   CALM   STRESSED   SAD   TIRED

SELF-CARE:

☐ DID I SLEEP WELL?

☐ DID I EAT NOURISHING FOODS?

☐ DOES MY COMPRESSION GARMENT FIT NICE & SNUG?

☐ ARE MY INCISIONS HEALING PROPERLY?

☐ HAS MY MOBILITY IMPROVED TODAY?

MY WATER INTAKE

EACH DROP REPRESENT 16 OUNCES.
80 OUNCES IS RECOMMENDED PER DAY.

⬦ ⬦ ⬦ ⬦ ⬦ ⬦ ⬦

NOTES

Reflection

What advice/words of encouragement would you give someone who is considering undergoing the same procedure?

_____

_____

_____

_____

_____

_____

I deserve happiness.

Recovery Day 8

HOW I FEEL TODAY

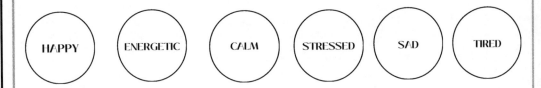

(HAPPY) (ENERGETIC) (CALM) (STRESSED) (SAD) (TIRED)

SELF-CARE:

☐ DID I SLEEP WELL?

☐ DID I EAT NOURISHING FOODS?

☐ DOES MY COMPRESSION GARMENT FIT NICE & SNUG?

☐ ARE MY INCISIONS HEALING PROPERLY?

☐ HAS MY MOBILITY IMPROVED TODAY?

MY WATER INTAKE

EACH DROP REPRESENT 16 OUNCES.
80 OUNCES IS RECOMMENDED PER DAY.

NOTES

Reflection

Reflect on a time when you confronted any negative self-talk or self-doubt. How can you replace it with positive self-affirming thoughts?

_____

_____

_____

_____

_____

_____

I can get through anything.

Recovery Day 9

HOW I FEEL TODAY

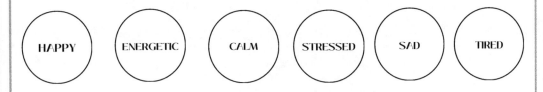

(HAPPY) (ENERGETIC) (CALM) (STRESSED) (SAD) (TIRED)

SELF-CARE:

☐ DID I SLEEP WELL?

☐ DID I EAT NOURISHING FOODS?

☐ DOES MY COMPRESSION GARMENT FIT NICE & SNUG?

☐ ARE MY INCISIONS HEALING PROPERLY?

☐ HAS MY MOBILITY IMPROVED TODAY?

MY WATER INTAKE

EACH DROP REPRESENT 16 OUNCES.
80 OUNCES IS RECOMMENDED PER DAY.

◇◇◇◇◇◇◇

NOTES

Reflection

Describe a particular moment when you felt overwhelmed by the recovery process. How did you overcome that feeling?

_____

_____

_____

_____

_____

_____

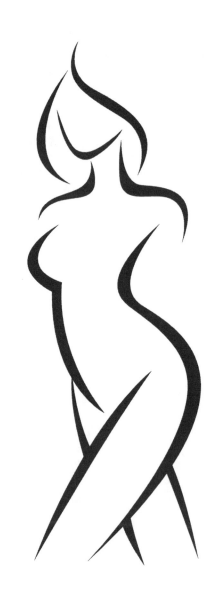

I see abundance all around me.

Recovery Day 10

HOW I FEEL TODAY

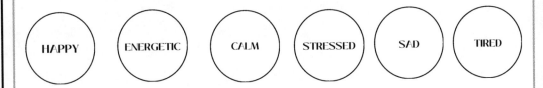

| HAPPY | ENERGETIC | CALM | STRESSED | SAD | TIRED |

SELF-CARE:

☐ DID I SLEEP WELL?

☐ DID I EAT NOURISHING FOODS?

☐ DOES MY COMPRESSION GARMENT FIT NICE & SNUG?

☐ ARE MY INCISIONS HEALING PROPERLY?

☐ HAS MY MOBILITY IMPROVED TODAY?

MY WATER INTAKE

EACH DROP REPRESENT 16 OUNCES. 80 OUNCES IS RECOMMENDED PER DAY.

⬡⬡⬡⬡⬡⬡

NOTES

Reflection

Think about the compliments or positive feedback you've received since your surgery. How can you internalize and believe in these affirmations?

_____

_____

_____

_____

_____

_____

I am brave.

Recovery
Day 11

Date
____/____/____

HOW I FEEL TODAY

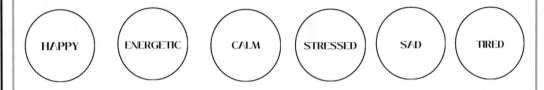

HAPPY   ENERGETIC   CALM   STRESSED   SAD   TIRED

SELF-CARE:

☐ DID I SLEEP WELL?

☐ DID I EAT NOURISHING FOODS?

☐ DOES MY COMPRESSION GARMENT FIT NICE & SNUG?

☐ ARE MY INCISIONS HEALING PROPERLY?

☐ HAS MY MOBILITY IMPROVED TODAY?

MY WATER INTAKE

*EACH DROP REPRESENT 16 OUNCES.
80 OUNCES IS RECOMMENDED PER DAY.*

NOTES

Reflection

Write about a supportive person/community who has helped you during your recovery. How do you lean on them for support and express gratitude?

_____

_____

_____

_____

_____

_____

I am amazing.

Recovery Day 12

Date
____/____/____

HOW I FEEL TODAY

(HAPPY) (ENERGETIC) (CALM) (STRESSED) (SAD) (TIRED)

SELF-CARE:

☐ DID I SLEEP WELL?

☐ DID I EAT NOURISHING FOODS?

☐ DOES MY COMPRESSION GARMENT FIT NICE & SNUG?

☐ ARE MY INCISIONS HEALING PROPERLY?

☐ HAS MY MOBILITY IMPROVED TODAY?

MY WATER INTAKE

EACH DROP REPRESENT 16 OUNCES.
80 OUNCES IS RECOMMENDED PER DAY.

◊ ◊ ◊ ◊ ◊ ◊ ◊

NOTES

Reflection

Write about any comparisons you've made with others during your recovery. How can you embrace your unique journey?

_____

_____

_____

_____

_____

_____

I am talented.

Recovery Day 13

HOW I FEEL TODAY

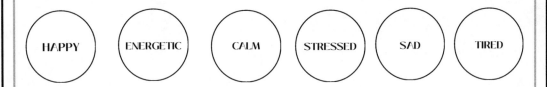

HAPPY · ENERGETIC · CALM · STRESSED · SAD · TIRED

SELF-CARE:

☐ DID I SLEEP WELL?

☐ DID I EAT NOURISHING FOODS?

☐ DOES MY COMPRESSION GARMENT FIT NICE & SNUG?

☐ ARE MY INCISIONS HEALING PROPERLY?

☐ HAS MY MOBILITY IMPROVED TODAY?

MY WATER INTAKE

EACH DROP REPRESENT 16 OUNCES. 80 OUNCES IS RECOMMENDED PER DAY.

◊ ◊ ◊ ◊ ◊ ◊ ◊

NOTES

Reflection

Reflect on a moment of vulnerability that you shared your recovery experience with someone else. How did it feel and what did you learn?

_____

_____

_____

_____

_____

_____

I am powerful.

Recovery Day 14

Date
____/____/____

HOW I FEEL TODAY

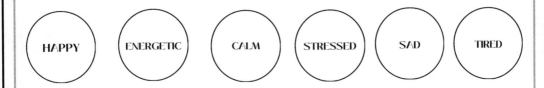

HAPPY · ENERGETIC · CALM · STRESSED · SAD · TIRED

SELF-CARE:

☐ DID I SLEEP WELL?

☐ DID I EAT NOURISHING FOODS?

☐ DOES MY COMPRESSION GARMENT FIT NICE & SNUG?

☐ ARE MY INCISIONS HEALING PROPERLY?

☐ HAS MY MOBILITY IMPROVED TODAY?

MY WATER INTAKE

*EACH DROP REPRESENT 16 OUNCES.
80 OUNCES IS RECOMMENDED PER DAY.*

NOTES

Reflection

What coping mechanisms or relaxation techniques helped manage stress during your recovery? How can you utilize it regularly?

_____

_____

_____

_____

_____

_____

I accept who I am.

Recovery Day 15

HOW I FEEL TODAY

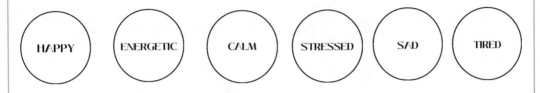

HAPPY ENERGETIC CALM STRESSED SAD TIRED

SELF-CARE:

☐ DID I SLEEP WELL?

☐ DID I EAT NOURISHING FOODS?

☐ DOES MY COMPRESSION GARMENT FIT NICE & SNUG?

☐ ARE MY INCISIONS HEALING PROPERLY?

☐ HAS MY MOBILITY IMPROVED TODAY?

MY WATER INTAKE

EACH DROP REPRESENT 16 OUNCES. 80 OUNCES IS RECOMMENDED PER DAY.

⬡⬡⬡⬡⬡⬡⬡

NOTES

Reflection

What obstacles have you encountered during your recovery? How can you maintain resilience in the face of adversity?

_____

_____

_____

_____

_____

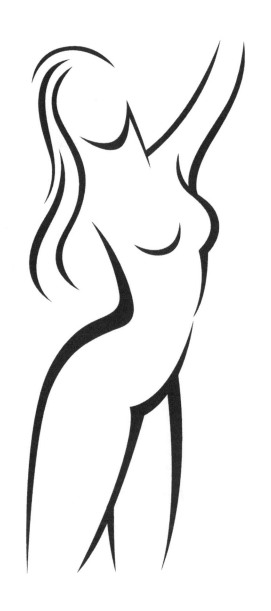

I am confident.

Recovery Day 16

HOW I FEEL TODAY

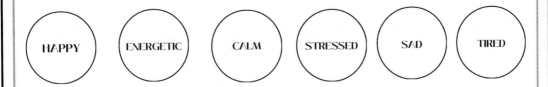

HAPPY   ENERGETIC   CALM   STRESSED   SAD   TIRED

SELF-CARE:

☐ DID I SLEEP WELL?

☐ DID I EAT NOURISHING FOODS?

☐ DOES MY COMPRESSION GARMENT FIT NICE & SNUG?

☐ ARE MY INCISIONS HEALING PROPERLY?

☐ HAS MY MOBILITY IMPROVED TODAY?

MY WATER INTAKE

EACH DROP REPRESENT 16 OUNCES. 80 OUNCES IS RECOMMENDED PER DAY.

◊ ◊ ◊ ◊ ◊ ◊

NOTES

Reflection

Write about a physical or emotional milestone you've reached during your recovery. How can you acknowledge and celebrate that achievement?

_____

_____

_____

_____

_____

_____

I do not chase, I attract.

Recovery Day 17

Date
___/___/___

HOW I FEEL TODAY

(HAPPY) (ENERGETIC) (CALM) (STRESSED) (SAD) (TIRED)

SELF-CARE:

☐ DID I SLEEP WELL?

☐ DID I EAT NOURISHING FOODS?

☐ DOES MY COMPRESSION GARMENT FIT NICE & SNUG?

☐ ARE MY INCISIONS HEALING PROPERLY?

☐ HAS MY MOBILITY IMPROVED TODAY?

MY WATER INTAKE

EACH DROP REPRESENT 16 OUNCES. 80 OUNCES IS RECOMMENDED PER DAY.

◇ ◇ ◇ ◇ ◇ ◇ ◇

NOTES

Reflection

Reflect on a particular moment when you embraced imperfections and saw unique strengths. How can you continue to celebrate your uniqueness?

_____

_____

_____

_____

_____

_____

I am creative.

Recovery Day 18

HOW I FEEL TODAY

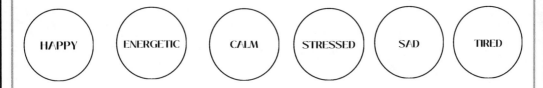

(HAPPY) (ENERGETIC) (CALM) (STRESSED) (SAD) (TIRED)

SELF-CARE:

☐ DID I SLEEP WELL?

☐ DID I EAT NOURISHING FOODS?

☐ DOES MY COMPRESSION GARMENT FIT NICE & SNUG?

☐ ARE MY INCISIONS HEALING PROPERLY?

☐ HAS MY MOBILITY IMPROVED TODAY?

MY WATER INTAKE

EACH DROP REPRESENT 16 OUNCES. 80 OUNCES IS RECOMMENDED PER DAY.

◇ ◇ ◇ ◇ ◇ ◇ ◇

NOTES

Reflection

What are some self-care rituals that bring you comfort during your recovery? Focus on what you CAN do instead of your restrictions.

_____

_____

_____

_____

_____

_____

I am successful.

Recovery Day 19

HOW I FEEL TODAY

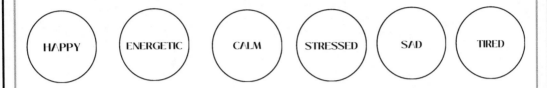

HAPPY   ENERGETIC   CALM   STRESSED   SAD   TIRED

SELF-CARE:

☐ **DID I SLEEP WELL?**

☐ **DID I EAT NOURISHING FOODS?**

☐ **DOES MY COMPRESSION GARMENT FIT NICE & SNUG?**

☐ **ARE MY INCISIONS HEALING PROPERLY?**

☐ **HAS MY MOBILITY IMPROVED TODAY?**

MY WATER INTAKE

EACH DROP REPRESENT 16 OUNCES. 80 OUNCES IS RECOMMENDED PER DAY.

NOTES

Reflection

Reflect on a specific moment after your surgery where you felt a surge of self-confidence. How can you maintain or nurture that feeling?.

_____

_____

_____

_____

_____

_____

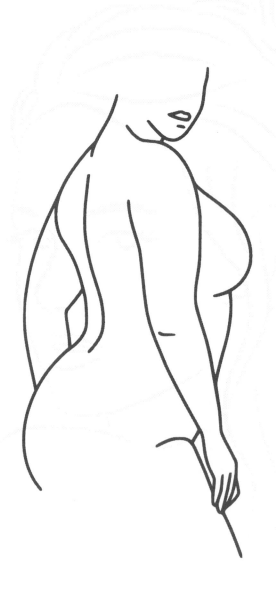

I am radiant.

Recovery Day 20

Date ___/___/___

HOW I FEEL TODAY

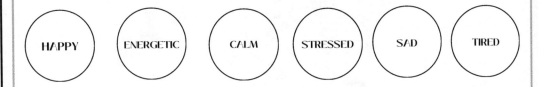

HAPPY ENERGETIC CALM STRESSED SAD TIRED

SELF-CARE:

☐ DID I SLEEP WELL?

☐ DID I EAT NOURISHING FOODS?

☐ DOES MY COMPRESSION GARMENT FIT NICE & SNUG?

☐ ARE MY INCISIONS HEALING PROPERLY?

☐ HAS MY MOBILITY IMPROVED TODAY?

MY WATER INTAKE

EACH DROP REPRESENT 16 OUNCES. 80 OUNCES IS RECOMMENDED PER DAY.

⬯⬯⬯⬯⬯⬯⬯

NOTES

Reflection

Picture your ideal vision of yourself post-recovery. How will you work towards achieving that vision?

_____

_____

_____

_____

_____

I am proud of who I am.

Recovery Day 21

Date ____/____/____

HOW I FEEL TODAY

(HAPPY) (ENERGETIC) (CALM) (STRESSED) (SAD) (TIRED)

SELF-CARE:

☐ DID I SLEEP WELL?

☐ DID I EAT NOURISHING FOODS?

☐ DOES MY COMPRESSION GARMENT FIT NICE & SNUG?

☐ ARE MY INCISIONS HEALING PROPERLY?

☐ HAS MY MOBILITY IMPROVED TODAY?

MY WATER INTAKE

EACH DROP REPRESENT 16 OUNCES. 80 OUNCES IS RECOMMENDED PER DAY.

◊ ◊ ◊ ◊ ◊ ◊ ◊

NOTES

Reflection

Were there any skills/hobbies that you've rediscovered during your recovery? How did it bring you joy and fulfillment?

_____

_____

_____

_____

_____

_____

I love and embrace
all my curves.

Recovery Day 22

HOW I FEEL TODAY

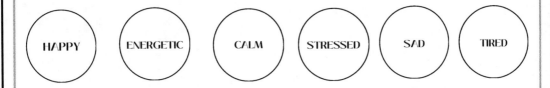

HAPPY   ENERGETIC   CALM   STRESSED   SAD   TIRED

SELF-CARE:

☐ DID I SLEEP WELL?

☐ DID I EAT NOURISHING FOODS?

☐ DOES MY COMPRESSION GARMENT FIT NICE & SNUG?

☐ ARE MY INCISIONS HEALING PROPERLY?

☐ HAS MY MOBILITY IMPROVED TODAY?

MY WATER INTAKE

EACH DROP REPRESENT 16 OUNCES.
80 OUNCES IS RECOMMENDED PER DAY.

NOTES

Reflection

Write about a routine or habit that has supported your healing process. How can you maintain it in your daily life?

_____

_____

_____

_____

_____

_____

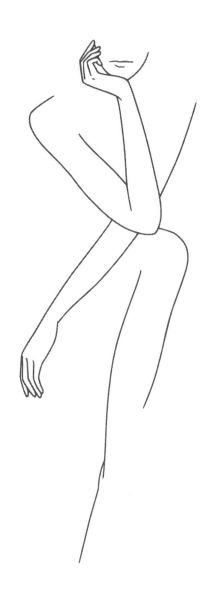

I am compassionate.

Recovery Day 23

HOW I FEEL TODAY

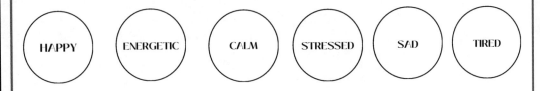

HAPPY   ENERGETIC   CALM   STRESSED   SAD   TIRED

SELF-CARE:

☐ DID I SLEEP WELL?

☐ DID I EAT NOURISHING FOODS?

☐ DOES MY COMPRESSION GARMENT FIT NICE & SNUG?

☐ ARE MY INCISIONS HEALING PROPERLY?

☐ HAS MY MOBILITY IMPROVED TODAY?

MY WATER INTAKE

EACH DROP REPRESENT 16 OUNCES.
80 OUNCES IS RECOMMENDED PER DAY.

NOTES

Reflection

Describe any emotional triggers that you've encountered post-surgery. How can you create a supportive environment during moments of vulnerability?

_____

_____

_____

_____

_____

_____

I am devoted to myself.

Recovery Day 24

HOW I FEEL TODAY

(HAPPY) (ENERGETIC) (CALM) (STRESSED) (SAD) (TIRED)

SELF-CARE:

☐ DID I SLEEP WELL?

☐ DID I EAT NOURISHING FOODS?

☐ DOES MY COMPRESSION GARMENT FIT NICE & SNUG?

☐ ARE MY INCISIONS HEALING PROPERLY?

☐ HAS MY MOBILITY IMPROVED TODAY?

MY WATER INTAKE

*EACH DROP REPRESENT 16 OUNCES.
80 OUNCES IS RECOMMENDED PER DAY.*

◊ ◊ ◊ ◊ ◊ ◊ ◊

NOTES

Reflection

Since your procedure, describe any positive changes you've noticed in your relationships. How can you nurture and maintain these positive connections?

_____

_____

_____

_____

_____

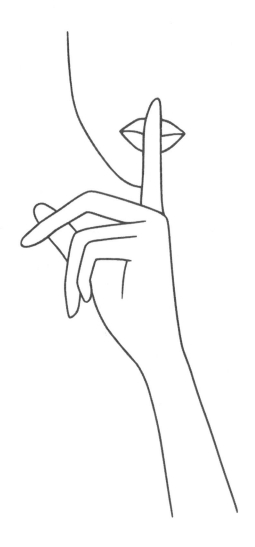

I am humble.

Recovery Day 25

HOW I FEEL TODAY

(HAPPY) (ENERGETIC) (CALM) (STRESSED) (SAD) (TIRED)

SELF-CARE:

☐ DID I SLEEP WELL?

☐ DID I EAT NOURISHING FOODS?

☐ DOES MY COMPRESSION GARMENT FIT NICE & SNUG?

☐ ARE MY INCISIONS HEALING PROPERLY?

☐ HAS MY MOBILITY IMPROVED TODAY?

MY WATER INTAKE

EACH DROP REPRESENT 16 OUNCES. 80 OUNCES IS RECOMMENDED PER DAY.

◊ ◊ ◊ ◊ ◊ ◊ ◊

NOTES

Reflection

Write about any areas of personal growth you've experienced during your recovery. How can you celebrate and build on that growth?

_____

_____

_____

_____

_____

_____

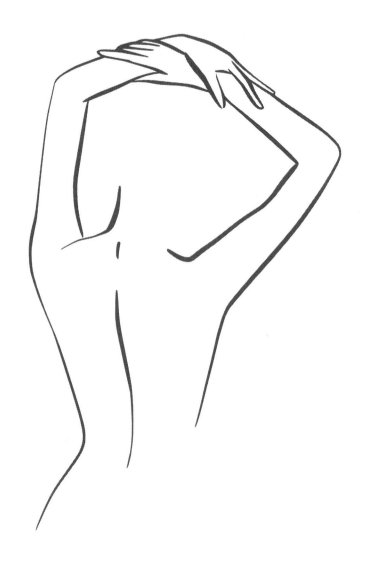

I am graceful.

Recovery Day 26

Date
_____ / _____ / _____

HOW I FEEL TODAY

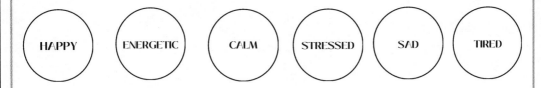

HAPPY   ENERGETIC   CALM   STRESSED   SAD   TIRED

SELF-CARE:

☐ **DID I SLEEP WELL?**

☐ **DID I EAT NOURISHING FOODS?**

☐ **DOES MY COMPRESSION GARMENT FIT NICE & SNUG?**

☐ **ARE MY INCISIONS HEALING PROPERLY?**

☐ **HAS MY MOBILITY IMPROVED TODAY?**

MY WATER INTAKE

EACH DROP REPRESENT 16 OUNCES.
80 OUNCES IS RECOMMENDED PER DAY.

NOTES

Reflection

Write a letter of gratitude to your body acknowledging it's resilience and strength during your recovery.

_____

_____

_____

_____

_____

_____

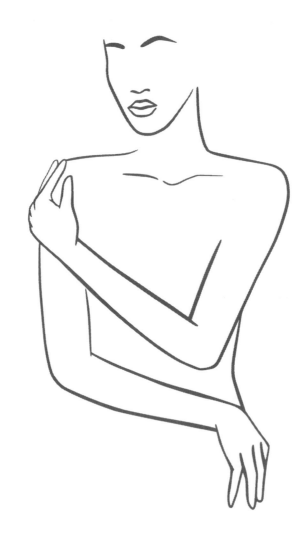

I am energetic.

Recovery
Day 27

Date
____/____/____

HOW I FEEL TODAY

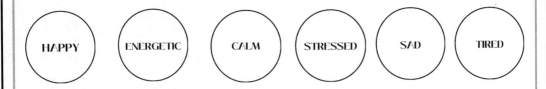

(HAPPY) (ENERGETIC) (CALM) (STRESSED) (SAD) (TIRED)

SELF-CARE:

☐ **DID I SLEEP WELL?**

☐ **DID I EAT NOURISHING FOODS?**

☐ **DOES MY COMPRESSION GARMENT FIT NICE & SNUG?**

☐ **ARE MY INCISIONS HEALING PROPERLY?**

☐ **HAS MY MOBILITY IMPROVED TODAY?**

MY WATER INTAKE

EACH DROP REPRESENT 16 OUNCES. 80 OUNCES IS RECOMMENDED PER DAY.

◊ ◊ ◊ ◊ ◊ ◊ ◊

NOTES

Reflection

Reflect on any moments of vulnerability or doubts you've faced while adjusting to post-surgery changes. How can you find acceptance and self-love in those moments?

_____

_____

_____

_____

_____

_____

_____

I am genuine.

Recovery Day 28

HOW I FEEL TODAY

| HAPPY | ENERGETIC | CALM | STRESSED | SAD | TIRED |

SELF-CARE:

☐ DID I SLEEP WELL?

☐ DID I EAT NOURISHING FOODS?

☐ DOES MY COMPRESSION GARMENT FIT NICE & SNUG?

☐ ARE MY INCISIONS HEALING PROPERLY?

☐ HAS MY MOBILITY IMPROVED TODAY?

MY WATER INTAKE

*EACH DROP REPRESENT 16 OUNCES.
80 OUNCES IS RECOMMENDED PER DAY.*

NOTES

Reflection

Reflect on a moment when you felt empowered to share your recovery journey with others. How did it impact your healing process?

_____

_____

_____

_____

_____

_____

I respect my body.

Recovery Day 29

Date
____/____/____

HOW I FEEL TODAY

(HAPPY) (ENERGETIC) (CALM) (STRESSED) (SAD) (TIRED)

SELF-CARE:

- ☐ DID I SLEEP WELL?
- ☐ DID I EAT NOURISHING FOODS?
- ☐ DOES MY COMPRESSION GARMENT FIT NICE & SNUG?
- ☐ ARE MY INCISIONS HEALING PROPERLY?
- ☐ HAS MY MOBILITY IMPROVED TODAY?

MY WATER INTAKE

EACH DROP REPRESENT 16 OUNCES. 80 OUNCES IS RECOMMENDED PER DAY.

◇ ◇ ◇ ◇ ◇ ◇ ◇

NOTES

Reflection

Envision a moment in the future when you'll confidently engage in activities you enjoy post-recovery. How can you work towards that moment?

_____

_____

_____

_____

_____

_____

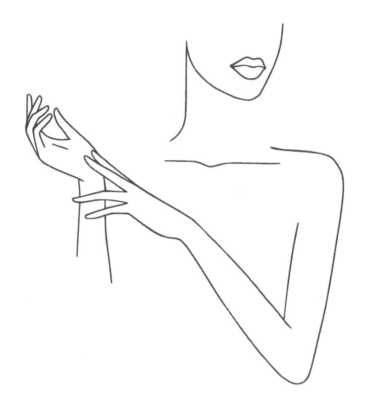

I forgive myself.

Recovery Day 30

HOW I FEEL TODAY

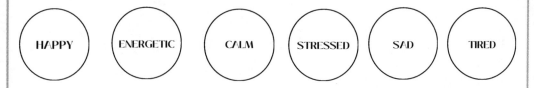

(HAPPY) (ENERGETIC) (CALM) (STRESSED) (SAD) (TIRED)

SELF-CARE:

☐ DID I SLEEP WELL?

☐ DID I EAT NOURISHING FOODS?

☐ DOES MY COMPRESSION GARMENT FIT NICE & SNUG?

☐ ARE MY INCISIONS HEALING PROPERLY?

☐ HAS MY MOBILITY IMPROVED TODAY?

MY WATER INTAKE

EACH DROP REPRESENT 16 OUNCES.
80 OUNCES IS RECOMMENDED PER DAY.

NOTES

Reflection

Think about any lessons you've learned about patience and self-compassion during your recovery. How can you apply these lessons in other aspects of your life?

_____

_____

_____

_____

_____

_____

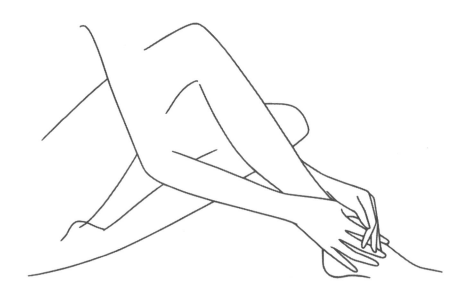

I am valuable.

Recovery Day 31

HOW I FEEL TODAY

HAPPY

ENERGETIC

CALM

STRESSED

SAD

TIRED

SELF-CARE:

☐ DID I SLEEP WELL?

☐ DID I EAT NOURISHING FOODS?

☐ DOES MY COMPRESSION GARMENT FIT NICE & SNUG?

☐ ARE MY INCISIONS HEALING PROPERLY?

☐ HAS MY MOBILITY IMPROVED TODAY?

MY WATER INTAKE

EACH DROP REPRESENT 16 OUNCES.
80 OUNCES IS RECOMMENDED PER DAY.

NOTES

Reflection

Write about a form of artistic expression or creative outlet that has been therapeutic during your recovery. How can you continue nurturing your creativity?

_____

_____

_____

_____

_____

_____

I am noble.

Recovery Day 32

HOW I FEEL TODAY

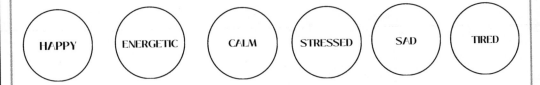

HAPPY   ENERGETIC   CALM   STRESSED   SAD   TIRED

SELF-CARE:

☐ DID I SLEEP WELL?

☐ DID I EAT NOURISHING FOODS?

☐ DOES MY COMPRESSION GARMENT FIT NICE & SNUG?

☐ ARE MY INCISIONS HEALING PROPERLY?

☐ HAS MY MOBILITY IMPROVED TODAY?

MY WATER INTAKE

EACH DROP REPRESENT 16 OUNCES.
80 OUNCES IS RECOMMENDED PER DAY.

NOTES

Reflection

Visualize a moment when you felt proud of your progress during your recovery. How can you celebrate your achievements along the way?

_____

_____

_____

_____

_____

_____

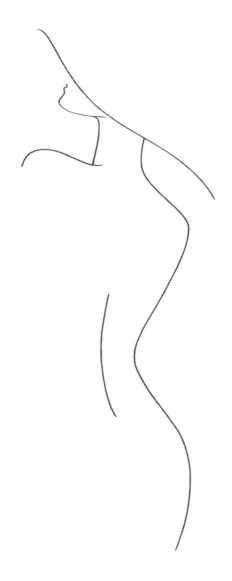

I am passionate.

Recovery Day 33

HOW I FEEL TODAY

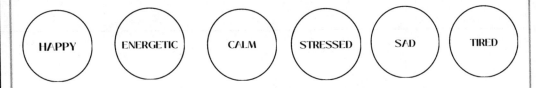

(HAPPY) (ENERGETIC) (CALM) (STRESSED) (SAD) (TIRED)

SELF-CARE:

☐ DID I SLEEP WELL?

☐ DID I EAT NOURISHING FOODS?

☐ DOES MY COMPRESSION GARMENT FIT NICE & SNUG?

☐ ARE MY INCISIONS HEALING PROPERLY?

☐ HAS MY MOBILITY IMPROVED TODAY?

MY WATER INTAKE

EACH DROP REPRESENT 16 OUNCES. 80 OUNCES IS RECOMMENDED PER DAY.

◇ ◇ ◇ ◇ ◇ ◇ ◇

NOTES

Reflection

Picture yourself as a strong and empowered individual, facing the world post-recovery. How can you maintain that sense of strength and power?

_____

_____

_____

_____

_____

_____

I am mindful.

Recovery
Day 34

HOW I FEEL TODAY

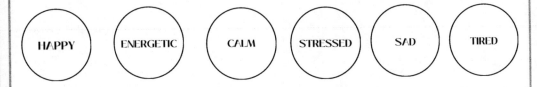

(HAPPY) (ENERGETIC) (CALM) (STRESSED) (SAD) (TIRED)

SELF-CARE:

☐ DID I SLEEP WELL?

☐ DID I EAT NOURISHING FOODS?

☐ DOES MY COMPRESSION GARMENT FIT NICE & SNUG?

☐ ARE MY INCISIONS HEALING PROPERLY?

☐ HAS MY MOBILITY IMPROVED TODAY?

MY WATER INTAKE

*EACH DROP REPRESENT 16 OUNCES.
80 OUNCES IS RECOMMENDED PER DAY.*

◇◇◇◇◇◇◇

NOTES

Reflection

Describe a moment when you felt comfortable and confident showing your vulnerability with others. How can you continue sharing your journey authentically?

_____

_____

_____

_____

_____

_____

I am optimistic.

Recovery
Day 35

HOW I FEEL TODAY

(HAPPY) (ENERGETIC) (CALM) (STRESSED) (SAD) (TIRED)

SELF-CARE:

☐ DID I SLEEP WELL?

☐ DID I EAT NOURISHING FOODS?

☐ DOES MY COMPRESSION GARMENT FIT NICE & SNUG?

☐ ARE MY INCISIONS HEALING PROPERLY?

☐ HAS MY MOBILITY IMPROVED TODAY?

MY WATER INTAKE

*EACH DROP REPRESENT 16 OUNCES.
80 OUNCES IS RECOMMENDED PER DAY.*

◇ ◇ ◇ ◇ ◇ ◇ ◇

NOTES

Reflection

Reflect on a moment when you found joy in the simple pleasures of life during your recovery. How can you continue savoring these moments?

_____

_____

_____

_____

_____

_____

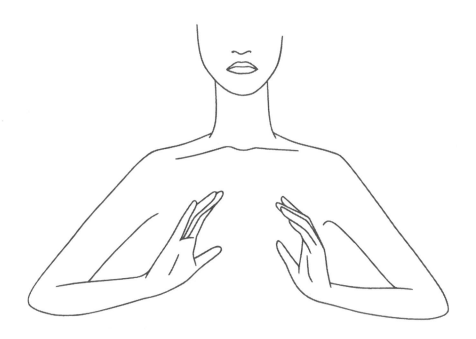

I am prosperous.

Recovery Day 36

HOW I FEEL TODAY

(HAPPY) (ENERGETIC) (CALM) (STRESSED) (SAD) (TIRED)

SELF-CARE:

☐ DID I SLEEP WELL?

☐ DID I EAT NOURISHING FOODS?

☐ DOES MY COMPRESSION GARMENT FIT NICE & SNUG?

☐ ARE MY INCISIONS HEALING PROPERLY?

☐ HAS MY MOBILITY IMPROVED TODAY?

MY WATER INTAKE

EACH DROP REPRESENT 16 OUNCES. 80 OUNCES IS RECOMMENDED PER DAY.

◊ ◊ ◊ ◊ ◊ ◊ ◊

NOTES

Reflection

List three things that you love about your new body and how it enriches your life.

_____

_____

_____

_____

_____

_____

I am proactive.

Recovery Day 37

Date ____/____/____

HOW I FEEL TODAY

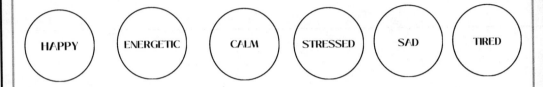

HAPPY — ENERGETIC — CALM — STRESSED — SAD — TIRED

SELF-CARE:

☐ DID I SLEEP WELL?

☐ DID I EAT NOURISHING FOODS?

☐ DOES MY COMPRESSION GARMENT FIT NICE & SNUG?

☐ ARE MY INCISIONS HEALING PROPERLY?

☐ HAS MY MOBILITY IMPROVED TODAY?

MY WATER INTAKE

EACH DROP REPRESENT 16 OUNCES.
80 OUNCES IS RECOMMENDED PER DAY.

◇◇◇◇◇◇◇

NOTES

Reflection

Write down three compliments you often receive and take a moment to appreciate them genuinely.

_____

_____

_____

_____

_____

_____

I am alluring.

Recovery Day 38

Date
___/___/___

HOW I FEEL TODAY

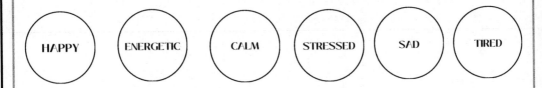

HAPPY   ENERGETIC   CALM   STRESSED   SAD   TIRED

SELF-CARE:

☐ DID I SLEEP WELL?

☐ DID I EAT NOURISHING FOODS?

☐ DOES MY COMPRESSION GARMENT FIT NICE & SNUG?

☐ ARE MY INCISIONS HEALING PROPERLY?

☐ HAS MY MOBILITY IMPROVED TODAY?

MY WATER INTAKE

EACH DROP REPRESENT 16 OUNCES.
80 OUNCES IS RECOMMENDED PER DAY.

NOTES

Reflection

Write about a moment in recovery when you tackled a difficult task and accomplished it with determination.

_____

_____

_____

_____

_____

_____

I am absolutely
gorgeous.

Recovery Day 39

HOW I FEEL TODAY

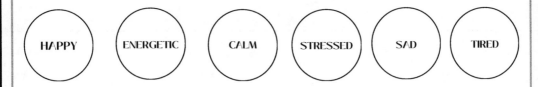

HAPPY ENERGETIC CALM STRESSED SAD TIRED

SELF-CARE:

☐ DID I SLEEP WELL?

☐ DID I EAT NOURISHING FOODS?

☐ DOES MY COMPRESSION GARMENT FIT NICE & SNUG?

☐ ARE MY INCISIONS HEALING PROPERLY?

☐ HAS MY MOBILITY IMPROVED TODAY?

MY WATER INTAKE

EACH DROP REPRESENT 16 OUNCES. 80 OUNCES IS RECOMMENDED PER DAY.

NOTES

Reflection

Describe some ways you can build a strong support system and surround yourself with positive influences.

_____

_____

_____

_____

_____

_____

I am an
extraordinary being.

Recovery
Day 40

Date
____/____/____

HOW I FEEL TODAY

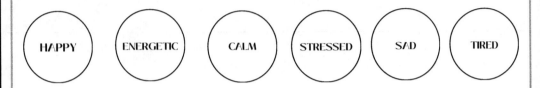

HAPPY ENERGETIC CALM STRESSED SAD TIRED

SELF-CARE:

☐ DID I SLEEP WELL?

☐ DID I EAT NOURISHING FOODS?

☐ DOES MY COMPRESSION GARMENT FIT NICE & SNUG?

☐ ARE MY INCISIONS HEALING PROPERLY?

☐ HAS MY MOBILITY IMPROVED TODAY?

MY WATER INTAKE

EACH DROP REPRESENT 16 OUNCES. 80 OUNCES IS RECOMMENDED PER DAY.

NOTES

Reflection

What are some ways you can maintain a positive mindset during your recovery?

_____

_____

_____

_____

_____

_____

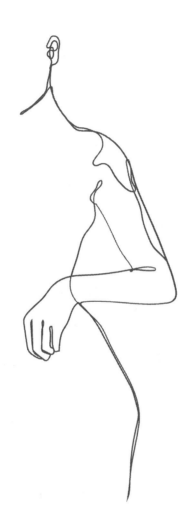

I am surrounded by positive energy.

Recovery Day 41

HOW I FEEL TODAY

HAPPY   ENERGETIC   CALM   STRESSED   SAD   TIRED

SELF-CARE:

☐ DID I SLEEP WELL?

☐ DID I EAT NOURISHING FOODS?

☐ DOES MY COMPRESSION GARMENT FIT NICE & SNUG?

☐ ARE MY INCISIONS HEALING PROPERLY?

☐ HAS MY MOBILITY IMPROVED TODAY?

MY WATER INTAKE

EACH DROP REPRESENT 16 OUNCES.
80 OUNCES IS RECOMMENDED PER DAY.

NOTES

Reflection

Name three unique qualities about yourself that make you special.

_____

_____

_____

_____

_____

_____

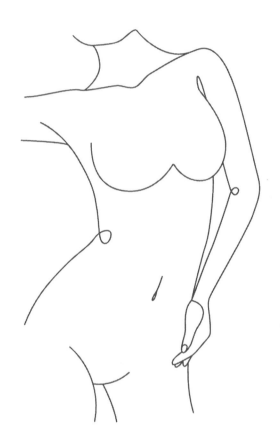

I am self-assured.

Recovery
Day 42

Date
____/____/____

HOW I FEEL TODAY

(HAPPY) (ENERGETIC) (CALM) (STRESSED) (SAD) (TIRED)

SELF-CARE:

☐ DID I SLEEP WELL?

☐ DID I EAT NOURISHING FOODS?

☐ DOES MY COMPRESSION GARMENT FIT NICE & SNUG?

☐ ARE MY INCISIONS HEALING PROPERLY?

☐ HAS MY MOBILITY IMPROVED TODAY?

MY WATER INTAKE

EACH DROP REPRESENT 16 OUNCES.
80 OUNCES IS RECOMMENDED PER DAY.

◇ ◇ ◇ ◇ ◇ ◇ ◇

NOTES

Reflection

Describe any challenges you're currently facing during your recovery and visualize yourself overcoming it with unwavering self-belief.

_____

_____

_____

_____

_____

_____

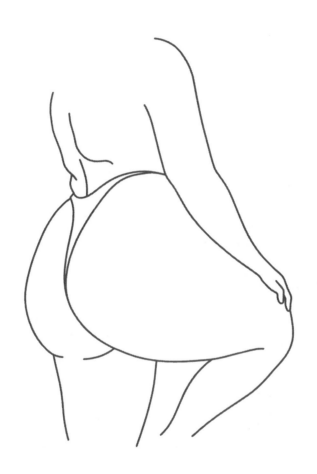

I accept and embrace
all of me.

Recovery Day 43

HOW I FEEL TODAY

(HAPPY) (ENERGETIC) (CALM) (STRESSED) (SAD) (TIRED)

SELF-CARE:

☐ DID I SLEEP WELL?

☐ DID I EAT NOURISHING FOODS?

☐ DOES MY COMPRESSION GARMENT FIT NICE & SNUG?

☐ ARE MY INCISIONS HEALING PROPERLY?

☐ HAS MY MOBILITY IMPROVED TODAY?

MY WATER INTAKE

EACH DROP REPRESENT 16 OUNCES. 80 OUNCES IS RECOMMENDED PER DAY.

◊ ◊ ◊ ◊ ◊ ◊ ◊

NOTES

Reflection

Write down five things you love about yourself, both inwardly and outwardly, and appreciate each one.

_____

_____

_____

_____

_____

_____

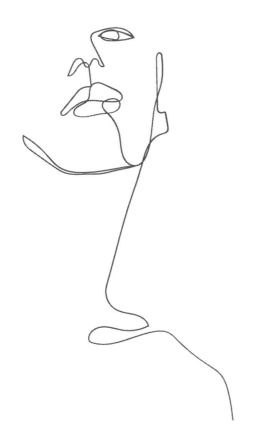

I take care of myself.

Recovery
Day 44

HOW I FEEL TODAY

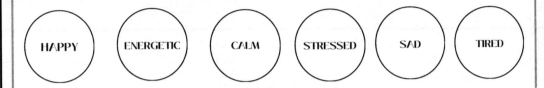

(HAPPY) (ENERGETIC) (CALM) (STRESSED) (SAD) (TIRED)

SELF-CARE:

☐ DID I SLEEP WELL?

☐ DID I EAT NOURISHING
  FOODS?

☐ DOES MY COMPRESSION
  GARMENT FIT NICE & SNUG?

☐ ARE MY INCISIONS HEALING
  PROPERLY?

☐ HAS MY MOBILITY IMPROVED
  TODAY?

MY WATER INTAKE

*EACH DROP REPRESENT 16 OUNCES.
80 OUNCES IS RECOMMENDED PER DAY.*

◇ ◇ ◇ ◇ ◇ ◇ ◇

NOTES

Reflection

What pain management techniques have worked for you during your
recovery? What advice would you give to those experiencing the same
discomfort?

_____

_____

_____

_____

_____

_____

I am accomplished.

Recovery Day 45

HOW I FEEL TODAY

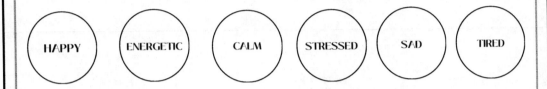

HAPPY **ENERGETIC** **CALM** **STRESSED** **SAD** **TIRED**

SELF-CARE:

☐ DID I SLEEP WELL?

☐ DID I EAT NOURISHING FOODS?

☐ DOES MY COMPRESSION GARMENT FIT NICE & SNUG?

☐ ARE MY INCISIONS HEALING PROPERLY?

☐ HAS MY MOBILITY IMPROVED TODAY?

MY WATER INTAKE

EACH DROP REPRESENT 16 OUNCES. 80 OUNCES IS RECOMMENDED PER DAY.

NOTES

Reflection

Even in the midst of recovery, what are some aspects of your life you are grateful for?

_____

_____

_____

_____

_____

_____

I am good to myself.

Recovery
Day 46

HOW I FEEL TODAY

(HAPPY) (ENERGETIC) (CALM) (STRESSED) (SAD) (TIRED)

SELF-CARE:

☐ DID I SLEEP WELL?

☐ DID I EAT NOURISHING FOODS?

☐ DOES MY COMPRESSION GARMENT FIT NICE & SNUG?

☐ ARE MY INCISIONS HEALING PROPERLY?

☐ HAS MY MOBILITY IMPROVED TODAY?

MY WATER INTAKE

EACH DROP REPRESENT 16 OUNCES. 80 OUNCES IS RECOMMENDED PER DAY.

◊ ◊ ◊ ◊ ◊ ◊ ◊

NOTES

Reflection

What physical changes have you noticed up until this point of recovery and how do they make you feel?

_____

_____

_____

_____

_____

_____

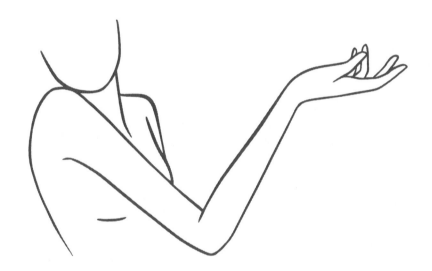

I am remarkable.

Recovery Day 47

HOW I FEEL TODAY

HAPPY   ENERGETIC   CALM   STRESSED   SAD   TIRED

SELF-CARE:

- ☐ DID I SLEEP WELL?
- ☐ DID I EAT NOURISHING FOODS?
- ☐ DOES MY COMPRESSION GARMENT FIT NICE & SNUG?
- ☐ ARE MY INCISIONS HEALING PROPERLY?
- ☐ HAS MY MOBILITY IMPROVED TODAY?

MY WATER INTAKE

EACH DROP REPRESENT 16 OUNCES.
80 OUNCES IS RECOMMENDED PER DAY.

NOTES

Reflection

What thoughts and feelings were you experiencing during the moments leading up to your surgery?

_____

_____

_____

_____

_____

_____

I believe in myself.

Recovery Day 48

Date
___ / ___ / ___

HOW I FEEL TODAY

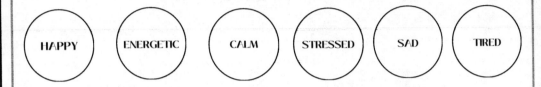

HAPPY   ENERGETIC   CALM   STRESSED   SAD   TIRED

SELF-CARE:

☐ DID I SLEEP WELL?

☐ DID I EAT NOURISHING FOODS?

☐ DOES MY COMPRESSION GARMENT FIT NICE & SNUG?

☐ ARE MY INCISIONS HEALING PROPERLY?

☐ HAS MY MOBILITY IMPROVED TODAY?

MY WATER INTAKE

EACH DROP REPRESENT 16 OUNCES.
80 OUNCES IS RECOMMENDED PER DAY.

◇◇◇◇◇◇◇

NOTES

Reflection

What was your initial reaction when you first saw the results of your surgery?

_____

_____

_____

_____

_____

_____

I am fulfilled.

Recovery
Day 49

HOW I FEEL TODAY

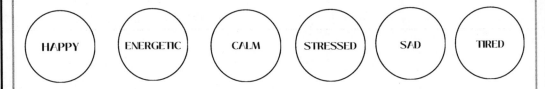

HAPPY   ENERGETIC   CALM   STRESSED   SAD   TIRED

SELF-CARE:

- ☐ DID I SLEEP WELL?

- ☐ DID I EAT NOURISHING FOODS?

- ☐ DOES MY COMPRESSION GARMENT FIT NICE & SNUG?

- ☐ ARE MY INCISIONS HEALING PROPERLY?

- ☐ HAS MY MOBILITY IMPROVED TODAY?

MY WATER INTAKE

*EACH DROP REPRESENT 16 OUNCES.
80 OUNCES IS RECOMMENDED PER DAY.*

◊◊◊◊◊◊◊

NOTES

Reflection

Contemplate the reactions of others to your cosmetic surgery. How do you handle questions or comments from family, friends, or acquaintances?

_____

_____

_____

_____

_____

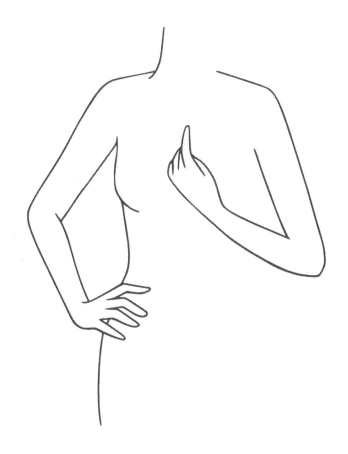

I am proud of myself.

Recovery Day 50

HOW I FEEL TODAY

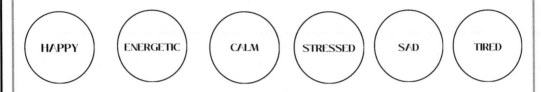

| HAPPY | ENERGETIC | CALM | STRESSED | SAD | TIRED |

SELF-CARE:

☐ DID I SLEEP WELL?

☐ DID I EAT NOURISHING FOODS?

☐ DOES MY COMPRESSION GARMENT FIT NICE & SNUG?

☐ ARE MY INCISIONS HEALING PROPERLY?

☐ HAS MY MOBILITY IMPROVED TODAY?

MY WATER INTAKE

EACH DROP REPRESENT 16 OUNCES. 80 OUNCES IS RECOMMENDED PER DAY.

◇◇◇◇◇◇◇

NOTES

Reflection

How do you feel today compared to the day of your surgery both physically and mentally?

_____

_____

_____

_____

_____

_____

I am content and
free from pain.

Recovery Day 51

HOW I FEEL TODAY

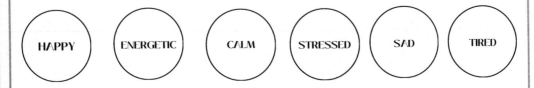

HAPPY   ENERGETIC   CALM   STRESSED   SAD   TIRED

SELF-CARE:

☐ **DID I SLEEP WELL?**

☐ **DID I EAT NOURISHING FOODS?**

☐ **DOES MY COMPRESSION GARMENT FIT NICE & SNUG?**

☐ **ARE MY INCISIONS HEALING PROPERLY?**

☐ **HAS MY MOBILITY IMPROVED TODAY?**

MY WATER INTAKE

EACH DROP REPRESENT 16 OUNCES. 80 OUNCES IS RECOMMENDED PER DAY.

NOTES

Reflection

What adjustments have you had to make since your surgery that were both challenging and beneficial?

_____

_____

_____

_____

_____

_____

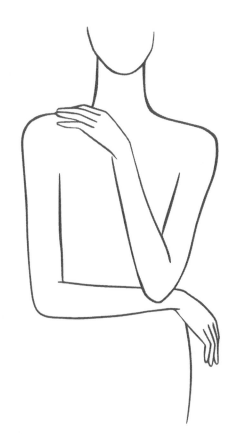

I am allowed to
feel good.

Recovery Day 52

Date
____/____/____

HOW I FEEL TODAY

(HAPPY) (ENERGETIC) (CALM) (STRESSED) (SAD) (TIRED)

SELF-CARE:

☐ **DID I SLEEP WELL?**

☐ **DID I EAT NOURISHING FOODS?**

☐ **DOES MY COMPRESSION GARMENT FIT NICE & SNUG?**

☐ **ARE MY INCISIONS HEALING PROPERLY?**

☐ **HAS MY MOBILITY IMPROVED TODAY?**

MY WATER INTAKE

EACH DROP REPRESENT 16 OUNCES. 80 OUNCES IS RECOMMENDED PER DAY.

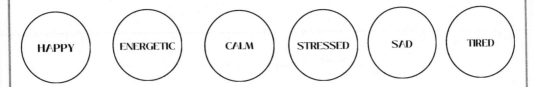

NOTES

Reflection

Explore the connection between physical health and mental well-being. How do these two aspects of your life intersect?

_____

_____

_____

_____

_____

_____

I am open to healing.

Recovery Day 53

HOW I FEEL TODAY

(HAPPY) (ENERGETIC) (CALM) (STRESSED) (SAD) (TIRED)

SELF-CARE:

☐ DID I SLEEP WELL?

☐ DID I EAT NOURISHING FOODS?

☐ DOES MY COMPRESSION GARMENT FIT NICE & SNUG?

☐ ARE MY INCISIONS HEALING PROPERLY?

☐ HAS MY MOBILITY IMPROVED TODAY?

MY WATER INTAKE

*EACH DROP REPRESENT 16 OUNCES.
80 OUNCES IS RECOMMENDED PER DAY.*

◊ ◊ ◊ ◊ ◊ ◊ ◊

NOTES

Reflection

What impact has this physical change had on your self–esteem and body image?

_____

_____

_____

_____

_____

I accept and embrace
my transformation.

Recovery Day 54

HOW I FEEL TODAY

(HAPPY) (ENERGETIC) (CALM) (STRESSED) (SAD) (TIRED)

SELF-CARE:

☐ DID I SLEEP WELL?

☐ DID I EAT NOURISHING FOODS?

☐ DOES MY COMPRESSION GARMENT FIT NICE & SNUG?

☐ ARE MY INCISIONS HEALING PROPERLY?

☐ HAS MY MOBILITY IMPROVED TODAY?

MY WATER INTAKE

*EACH DROP REPRESENT 16 OUNCES.
80 OUNCES IS RECOMMENDED PER DAY.*

NOTES

Reflection

How does your body image influence your self-esteem and self-worth? Be honest about any insecurities you may have.

_____

_____

_____

_____

_____

_____

I am more than just my
physical being.

Recovery Day 55

HOW I FEEL TODAY

(HAPPY)   (ENERGETIC)   (CALM)   (STRESSED)   (SAD)   (TIRED)

SELF-CARE:

☐ DID I SLEEP WELL?

☐ DID I EAT NOURISHING FOODS?

☐ DOES MY COMPRESSION GARMENT FIT NICE & SNUG?

☐ ARE MY INCISIONS HEALING PROPERLY?

☐ HAS MY MOBILITY IMPROVED TODAY?

MY WATER INTAKE

*EACH DROP REPRESENT 16 OUNCES.
80 OUNCES IS RECOMMENDED PER DAY.*

◊ ◊ ◊ ◊ ◊ ◊ ◊

NOTES

Reflection

How do you define beauty in yourself and others beyond physical appearance?

_____

_____

_____

_____

_____

_____

I will allow myself
to evolve.

Recovery Day 56

HOW I FEEL TODAY

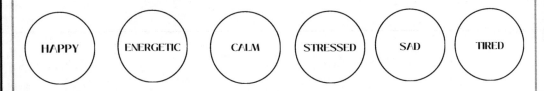

(HAPPY)   (ENERGETIC)   (CALM)   (STRESSED)   (SAD)   (TIRED)

SELF-CARE:

☐ DID I SLEEP WELL?

☐ DID I EAT NOURISHING FOODS?

☐ DOES MY COMPRESSION GARMENT FIT NICE & SNUG?

☐ ARE MY INCISIONS HEALING PROPERLY?

☐ HAS MY MOBILITY IMPROVED TODAY?

MY WATER INTAKE

EACH DROP REPRESENT 16 OUNCES.
80 OUNCES IS RECOMMENDED PER DAY.

◇ ◇ ◇ ◇ ◇ ◇ ◇

NOTES

Reflection

Describe how you felt about your body before the surgery. How has it evolved since then both physically and emotionally?

_____

_____

_____

_____

_____

_____

I am determined.

Recovery Day 57

HOW I FEEL TODAY

HAPPY ENERGETIC CALM STRESSED SAD TIRED

SELF-CARE:

☐ DID I SLEEP WELL?

☐ DID I EAT NOURISHING FOODS?

☐ DOES MY COMPRESSION GARMENT FIT NICE & SNUG?

☐ ARE MY INCISIONS HEALING PROPERLY?

☐ HAS MY MOBILITY IMPROVED TODAY?

MY WATER INTAKE

EACH DROP REPRESENT 16 OUNCES. 80 OUNCES IS RECOMMENDED PER DAY.

NOTES

Reflection

What has been the most challenging emotion to deal with during your recovery and how have you coped with it?

_____

_____

_____

_____

_____

_____

I trust my decisions.

Recovery Day 58

HOW I FEEL TODAY

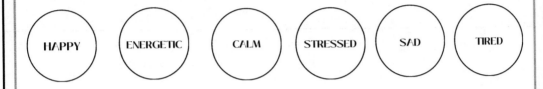

HAPPY   ENERGETIC   CALM   STRESSED   SAD   TIRED

SELF-CARE:

☐ DID I SLEEP WELL?

☐ DID I EAT NOURISHING FOODS?

☐ DOES MY COMPRESSION GARMENT FIT NICE & SNUG?

☐ ARE MY INCISIONS HEALING PROPERLY?

☐ HAS MY MOBILITY IMPROVED TODAY?

MY WATER INTAKE

*EACH DROP REPRESENT 16 OUNCES.
80 OUNCES IS RECOMMENDED PER DAY.*

NOTES

Reflection

What are your favorite ways to relax and unwind when you need a break from the challenges of recovery?

_____

_____

_____

_____

_____

_____

I can and I will.

Recovery Day 59

HOW I FEEL TODAY

(HAPPY) (ENERGETIC) (CALM) (STRESSED) (SAD) (TIRED)

SELF-CARE:

☐ DID I SLEEP WELL?

☐ DID I EAT NOURISHING FOODS?

☐ DOES MY COMPRESSION GARMENT FIT NICE & SNUG?

☐ ARE MY INCISIONS HEALING PROPERLY?

☐ HAS MY MOBILITY IMPROVED TODAY?

MY WATER INTAKE

EACH DROP REPRESENT 16 OUNCES. 80 OUNCES IS RECOMMENDED PER DAY.

NOTES

Reflection

What makes you feel empowered and confident, regardless of any physical changes?

_____

_____

_____

_____

_____

_____

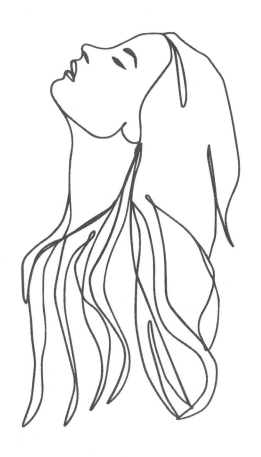

I am gifted.

Recovery Day 60

Date ___/___/___

HOW I FEEL TODAY

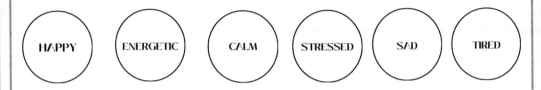

HAPPY | ENERGETIC | CALM | STRESSED | SAD | TIRED

SELF-CARE:

☐ DID I SLEEP WELL?

☐ DID I EAT NOURISHING FOODS?

☐ DOES MY COMPRESSION GARMENT FIT NICE & SNUG?

☐ ARE MY INCISIONS HEALING PROPERLY?

☐ HAS MY MOBILITY IMPROVED TODAY?

MY WATER INTAKE

EACH DROP REPRESENT 16 OUNCES. 80 OUNCES IS RECOMMENDED PER DAY.

NOTES

Reflection

Considering the knowledge that you have gained from this recovery process, would you do it over again? Why or why not?

_____

_____

_____

_____

_____

_____

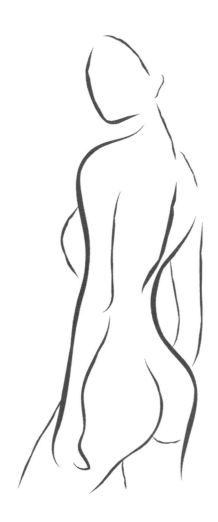

I am phenomenal.

Notes

Notes

Notes

Notes

Notes

Made in the USA
Columbia, SC
12 November 2023

25905746R10074